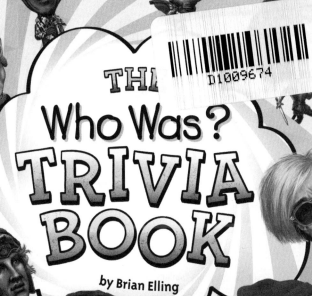

THE Who Was?
TRIVIA BOOK

by Brian Elling

Penguin Workshop

To Justin, William, and Olivia—BE

PENGUIN WORKSHOP
An imprint of Penguin Random House LLC, New York

First published in the United States of America by Penguin Workshop,
an imprint of Penguin Random House LLC, New York, 2022

Visit us online at penguinrandomhouse.com.

Library of Congress Cataloging-in-Publication Data is available.

Printed in the United States of America

ISBN 9780593222232   10 9 8 7 6 5 4 3 2 1 WOR

How much do you know about the most important people in world history?

Let's find out! Filled with hundreds of trivia questions, this book is your chance to show off all you know about everyone's favorite artists, activists, inventors, world leaders, authors, athletes, entertainers, and heroes. Test yourself, test your friends, and pick up a few new facts along the way!

Get ready to fill your brain with the most interesting information about the most impressive Who Was? subjects the world has ever known!

First, the First Ladies

Each of these presidential wives influenced American history in their own way! How much do you know about their accomplishments?

Why did Michelle Obama create a program called "Let's Move!"?

    a)   To teach children how to fold and pack cardboard boxes

    b)   To encourage children to hula dance

    c)   To inspire children to exercise

    d)   To help children ride their scooters safely

What did Abigail Adams do during the long periods of time when her husband was working far away?

    a)   Wrote letters to her husband that influenced American politics

    b)   Managed their home and farm

    c)   Sold goods to make a profit

    d)   All of the above

What acronym (nickname) is sometimes used for the First Ladies of the United States?

    a)   AWOL

    b)   FLOTUS

    c)   OSHA

    d)   YOLO

Hillary Clinton was the first First Lady *and* the first woman to . . .

a) Refuse to move out of the White House
b) Become the Democratic nominee for president
c) Write a best-selling book with her picture on it
d) Work for all Americans to get governmental health care

After her death in 1994, which landmark in New York City was renamed in honor of Jacqueline Kennedy's amazing life?

a) Grand Central Terminal
b) The Reservoir in Central Park
c) The Hudson River
d) The Statue of Happiness

Which war did *not* occur during Abigail Adams's lifetime?

a) The War of 1812
b) The American Revolution
c) The French Revolution
d) The War of the Tulips

When Jacqueline Kennedy moved into the White House, what was one of her priorities?

a) To install solar panels
b) To restore historic artifacts and put them on display
c) To create a secret tunnel to the Washington Monument
d) To build a half-pipe and declare April National Skateboarding Month

Who was the first First Lady to live in the White House?

a) Betsy Ross
b) Mrs. White
c) Abigail Adams
d) Eleanor Roosevelt

Which First Lady received a Presidential Medal of Freedom for her work as First Lady?

a) Betty Ford
b) Michelle Obama
c) Hillary Clinton
d) Eleanor Roosevelt

Which of these was *not* one of the many causes that Eleanor Roosevelt supported as First Lady?

a) Equal rights for all Americans
b) An end to poverty
c) President Roosevelt's reelection campaign
d) The need for a transcontinental railway

Which is *not* part of Jacqueline Kennedy's full name?

a) Bouvier
b) Strelka
c) Onassis
d) Lee

They Said What?

Can you tell which of these famous quotes from our Who Was? heroes are real and which are made-up?

Which is a well-known quote from the famous boxer Muhammad Ali?

a) "Float like a boat, sting like a jellyfish."

b) "Float like a butter knife, sting like a stingray."

c) "Float like a butterfly, sting like a bee."

d) "Float like a kite, bend like a knee."

What did Neil Armstrong say when he first stepped foot on the moon?

a) "The *Eagle* has landed."

b) "Houston, we have a problem."

c) "Ow! My ankle!"

d) "That's one small step for a man, one giant leap for mankind."

Which is one of Julius Caesar's famous phrases?

a) "I came, I saw, I collected taxes."

b) "I came, I slept late, I conquered."

c) "I came, I saw, I conquered."

d) "I am, I said, I conquered."

Which inspiring quote did Dolly Parton say?

a) "I refuse to settle for something less than great."

b) "It takes a lot of money to look this bedazzled."

c) "Make your dreams as tall as your hair."

d) "Sparkle and the world will sparkle with you."

Which famous quote did Bill Gates say after he founded Microsoft Corporation?

    a) "Woo-hoo! I'm rich!"

    b) "I believe that with great wealth comes great responsibility—a responsibility to give back to society."

    c) "A password a day keeps the computer virus away."

    d) "Never put off until tomorrow what you can make a computer do today."

Which is *not* one of Andy Warhol's famous quotes?

    a) "I like boring things."

    b) "An artist is someone who produces things that people don't need to have."

    c) "Art is what you can get at the supermarket."

    d) "Pop Art is for everyone."

Which is a famous line from one of Martin Luther King Jr.'s speeches?

    a) "Four score and seven years ago . . ."

    b) "I have a dream . . ."

    c) "To be or not to be . . ."

    d) "We shall go on to the end . . ."

What did Julia Child say at the end of each episode of her cooking show?

    a) "Le Magnifique!"

    b) "Bon appétit!"

    c) "Ciao for now!"

    d) "Until we eat again!"

What did Frida Kahlo respond to an art critic who said she was a surrealist painter?

   a) "I never painted dreams. I painted my own reality."

   b) "Actually, I'm a *surreally good* painter!"

   c) "Art is subjective."

   d) "Beauty is in the eyebrow of the beholder."

What did Alexander Graham Bell say when he made the first telephone call ever?

   a) "Eureka! We did it!"

   b) "Hold on. I have another call."

   c) "One small step for a man. One giant leap for telephones."

   d) "Mr. Watson—come here—I want to see you."

What was one of Steve Irwin's favorite phrases to say on his TV show *The Crocodile Hunter*?

   a) "Crikey!"

   b) "That's a real chomper!"

   c) "Here, crocky, crocky!"

   d) "See you in a while, crocodile."

Which of the below is a famous quote from President Franklin Roosevelt?

   a) "The only thing we have to fear is bad dreams."

   b) "The only thing we have to fear is fear itself."

   c) "The only thing we have to fear is forgetting to vote."

   d) "The only thing we have to fear is vampires."

Men of the Sea

When you're out at sea for months, there's plenty of time to learn lots of trivia. Let's hope you've been on a boat long enough to correctly answer these questions about great sailors!

The Norse explorer Leif Erikson and his family were . . .

a) Pirates
b) The French royalty
c) Vikings
d) Citizens of Atlantis

What was Blackbeard the pirate's real name?

a) Captain Jack Pigeon
b) Edward Teach
c) Sillius Black
d) Jolly Roger

Which one of these scientists is known for exploring the undersea world?

a) Albert Einstein
b) Sir Isaac Newton
c) Jacques Cousteau
d) Ernest Shackleton

Arrggggh! Blackbeard and his mateys used their ships to blockade the entrance to the harbor of Charles Town (now known as Charleston), South Carolina.

a) True
b) False

Why did sailors like Leif Erikson carve dragon heads onto the front of their ships?

a) To scare off sea monsters
b) To intimidate their enemies
c) To express their creative side
d) To attract dragons

What was the name of Jacques Cousteau's first award-winning documentary film?

a) *The Silent World*
b) *Water World*
c) *20,000 Leagues Under the Sea*
d) *I Found Nemo*

Who was the first European to travel to North America?

a) Christopher Columbus
b) Ferdinand Magellan
c) Leif Erikson
d) Captain America

Which of the below ships *wasn't* attacked by Blackbeard?

a) *The Revenge*
b) *La Concorde*
c) *The Margaret*
d) *Protestant Caesar*

Jacques Cousteau helped to protect the environment of Antarctica.

a) True
b) False

Where did Blackbeard and his pirates hide from the British Navy?

a) In barrels
b) Along the coast of North Carolina
c) In a hotel on Miami Beach
d) In the Tower of London

Which is *not* a weapon that Vikings may have used?

a) Javelin
b) Ax
c) Spear
d) Cannon

Which Writer Is Right?

So many incredible authors. And so many questions. Can you answer them all?

Which book was *not* written by J. K. Rowling?

- a) *Harry Potter and the Sorcerer's Stone*
- b) *Harry Potter and the Chamber of Gems*
- c) *Harry Potter and the Prisoner of Azkaban*
- d) *Harry Potter and the Goblet of Fire*

What is the name of one of Laura Ingalls Wilder's famous books?

- a) *Little Horse on the Prairie*
- b) *Little Women*
- c) *Little House on the Prairie*
- d) *Nothing Plain About the Great Plains*

Who is the author of the book *Charlie and the Chocolate Factory*?

- a) William Shakespeare
- b) Johnny Appleseed
- c) Roald Dahl
- d) Wilhelm Grimm

Maurice Sendak loved writing and designing sets for opera.

- a) True
- b) False

What famous book series was written by Jeff Kinney?

a) Diary of a Wimpy Kid
b) The Hobbit
c) Harry Potty
d) Little House on the Prairie

Which of the below is a book written by Charles Dickens?

a) *A Christmas Carol*
b) *The Lord of the Rings*
c) *Romeo and Juliet*
d) All of the above

Who wrote the book *Uncle Tom's Cabin*?

a) J. R. R. Tolkien
b) Coretta Scott King
c) Uncle Tom
d) Harriet Beecher Stowe

In the book *Little House on the Prairie*, what did author Laura Ingalls ride on when her family moved west?

a) A team of oxen
b) A covered wagon
c) A buffalo
d) All of the above

Which of the below is *not* a book written by Roald Dahl?

a) *James and the Rotten Peach*
b) *Charlie and the Chocolate Factory*
c) *Matilda*
d) *Fantastic Mr. Fox*

What did the Brothers Grimm do to gather fairy tales for their books?

a) Interviewed local people and wrote down the stories
b) Looked them up in old books in the library
c) Went to the woods to ask a witch
d) Traveled to France

Who is Greg Heffley?

a) A famous basketball player for the New York Knicks
b) A character in a series of books by Jeff Kinney
c) A character in *Where the Wild Things Are*
d) An explorer who mapped Antarctica

Which of the below is *not* a title of a Judy Blume book?

a) *Are You There God? It's Me, Margaret*
b) *Double Chocolate Fudge*
c) *Otherwise Known as Sheila the Great*
d) *Tales of a Fourth Grade Nothing*

Which of the below is *not* a book written by Dr. Seuss?

a) *The Cat in the Hat*
b) *Oh, the Places You'll Go!*
c) *Blue Eggs and Bacon*
d) *How the Grinch Stole Christmas*

Scientifically Speaking

Here's a quick experiment: Use these questions to accurately measure how much you know about the lives of these stunning scientists!

Which scientist is known for his theory of evolution?

a) Tommy Galapagos

b) Charles Darwin

c) Thomas Edison

d) Gene E. Ticks

What disease did George Washington Carver survive as a child?

a) Whooping cough

b) Bubonic plague

c) Scurvy

d) Acne

Which scientist is responsible for defining gravity and for discovering the nature of light?

a) Albert Einstein

b) Sir Isaac Newton

c) Galileo

d) Leonardo da Vinci

Which famous book about the origins of the universe was written by Stephen Hawking?

a) *A Brief History of Time*
b) *On the Origin of Species*
c) *Harry Potter and the Scientist's Stone*
d) *The World As I See It*

Jane Goodall spent many nights living alone in the jungles of Tanzania.

a) True
b) False

Which scientist wrote the equation E=mc²?

a) Alexander Graham Bell
b) Albert Einstein
c) Isaac Newton
d) Galileo

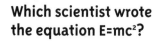

Which scientist is famous for realizing the sun does not circle the Earth?

a) Alexander Graham Bell

b) Albert Einstein

c) Jacques Cousteau

d) Galileo

When Marie Curie discovered the element polonium, what did she name it after?

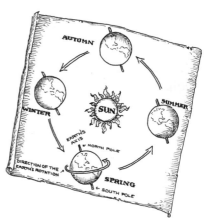

a) Poland

b) Water polo

c) Polar bears

d) Polio

What did Jane Goodall observe about chimpanzee behavior?

a) Chimpanzees use tools like humans.

b) Chimpanzees have amazing personalities.

c) Chimpanzees eat termites (and meat and plants).

d) All of the above

Which of the below is the name of an element discovered by Marie Curie?

a) Gymnasium

b) Radium

c) Helium

d) Terrarium

Which scientist showed people an eclipse to prove that light could bend around planets?

a) Albert Einstein
b) Isaac Newton
c) Galileo
d) Neil Armstrong

What islands did Charles Darwin visit to study evolution?

a) Hawaii
b) The Bahamas
c) The Galapagos
d) Antarctica

What historical event gave Isaac Newton lots of time alone to conduct experiments?

a) War with Spain
b) The Plague
c) The closing of the Royal Society
d) All of the above

Stephen Hawking suffered from ALS, a disease that caused him to lose the use of his arms and legs.

a) True
b) False

What natural phenomenon did Isaac Newton help explain by experimenting with prisms?

a) The tides
b) The full moon
c) Rainbows
d) The rotation of the Earth

Which scientist became famous for studying radioactive elements that glow in the dark?

a) Marie Curie
b) Ray Dium
c) Poe Lonium
d) Ray Donne

Who was the first Black professor at Iowa State Agricultural College?

a) George Washington Carver
b) Booker T. Washington
c) Alexander Hamilton
d) Sally Ride

What did Charles Darwin's theory of natural selection reveal?

a) That animals and plants compete for food
b) That animals and plants evolve slowly over time
c) That animals and plants have always been the same
d) That animals and plants are fun to keep as pets

Entertaining Trivia

Put your hands together and applaud for . . .
the right answers to these questions about our
most talented entertainers!

In Charlie Chaplin's time, what were "talkies"?

    a) Movies that allowed the audience to talk during the film

    b) Movies that played sound and images on the screen together

    c) Movies that didn't have music

    d) Movies that had a telephone call in them

Which of the below is *not* a movie or TV series made by Jim Henson?

    a) *The Dark Crystal*

    b) *Fraggle Rock*

    c) *The Muppet Movie*

    d) *The Empire Strikes Back*

Which of these famous characters did George Lucas create for *Star Wars*?

    a) E.T.

    b) Alf

    c) Princess Leia

    d) Wonder Woman

Who is known for exploring the world looking for unusual objects, facts, and people to be featured in his *Believe It or Not* cartoons, radio program, and TV show?

   a) Ferdinand Magellan
   b) Robert Ripley
   c) Christopher Columbus
   d) Johnny Appleseed

Which of the below wasn't one of Annie Oakley's daring acts?

   a) Scrambling eggs by shooting them while they were in the air
   b) Slicing a playing card in half by shooting at it
   c) Shooting a target while upside down
   d) Shooting a target while swimming underwater

Why did Bruce Lee first learn martial arts?

   a) To protect himself
   b) To compete for trophies
   c) To become famous
   d) As part of a healthy exercise routine

What was the name of Steve Irwin's TV show about nature?

   a) *The Hippo Hunter*
   b) *The Crocodile Hunter*
   c) *The Snake Whisperer*
   d) *The Australian Lizard Man*

George Lucas founded a special effects company called ILM. What does ILM stand for?

a) Instant Light & Magic
b) Industrial Light & Magic
c) Incredible Light & Movies
d) Imaginative Lightsaber Magic

Bruce Lee's strength and quickness helped him to do which of the below?

a) Perform kung fu
b) Dance the cha-cha
c) Star in movies and TV shows
d) All of the above

What did Ehrich Weiss change his name to when he decided to become a famous magician?

a) Mr. Magic!
b) Joe Disappearo
c) Penn Teller
d) Harry Houdini

Which was one of Harry Houdini's famous tricks?

a) The Vanishing Dinosaur Trick
b) The Brick Chimney Trick
c) The Vanishing Elephant Trick
d) The Disappearing Handcuffs Trick

Why did Harry Houdini go to Australia?

a) To pet a kangaroo
b) To escape from the inside of a crocodile
c) To be the first person to fly a plane in Australia
d) To buy stronger handcuffs for his act

Which celebrity actor starred in many George Lucas films?

a) Mickey Mouse
b) Harrison Ford
c) Steven Spielberg
d) Chewbacca

What famous quote did George Lucas write for the very first Star Wars movie?

a) "May the stars be with you."
b) "Yoda, I'm your father!"
c) "Beam me up, Scotty."
d) "May the Force be with you."

Which of the below is *not* one of the Three Stooges?

a) Larry
b) Moe
c) Curly
d) Squiggles

Military Might (Or Might Not)

Attention, soldiers! You've been enlisted to embark on a mission to answer questions about the world's most famous military leaders! *Forward march!*

Which of these military leaders became prime minister of Cuba beginning in 1959?

a) Ulysses S. Grant

b) Thomas Jefferson

c) Fidel Castro

d) Cesar Chavez

What was the name of the brave group of Black military pilots who fought in World War II?

a) The Dogfighters

b) The Tuskegee Airmen

c) The Blue Tails

d) The Flying Aces

Which British leader helped the United Kingdom survive World War II?

a) Ulysses S. Grant

b) Winston Churchill

c) Alfred Hitchcock

d) Harry S. Truman

Which French emperor lost the Battle of Waterloo?

a) King Louis the XIV
b) Joan of Arc
c) Napoleon Bonaparte
d) Louis Braille

What area of the world did Genghis Khan rule?

a) The Mongolian Steppe
b) Parts of China
c) The Khwārezm Empire
d) All of the above

Which one of these cities was *not* conquered by Alexander the Great?

a) Tyre
b) Fresno
c) Babylon
d) Gaza

What made Charles Hall famous during World War II?

a) He was the first Black pilot to shoot down a German war plane.

b) He was the first pilot to graduate from the Coffey School of Aviation.

c) He was the first pilot to meet Harry S. Truman.

d) He was the first pilot to write about Pearl Harbor.

Which city in Egypt was named after its famous conqueror?

a) Henria (by Henry VIII)

b) Khansas City (by Genghis Khan)

c) Alexandria (by Alexander the Great)

d) Caesarville (by Julius Caesar)

Why did Napoleon Bonaparte write a group of laws called the Napoleonic Code?

a) To establish that all male citizens of France were equal under the law

b) To make sure French food was served in all restaurants

c) To allow the French government to send secret messages

d) To establish a French national holiday in his honor

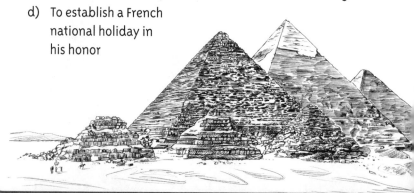

Let's Get Inventive

We've invented some questions about these amazing inventors. Can you invent some correct answers?

Who invented a coil that helped create the first transatlantic radio transmission?

a) Nikola Tesla

b) Orville Wright

c) Guglielmo Marconi

d) Samuel Morse

What type of invention is a decapoint?

a) A ten-beam laser pointer designed by Louis Braille

b) A backyard entertaining space designed by Louis Braille

c) A machine invented by Louis Braille to write in secret code

d) A form of the alphabet designed by Louis Braille that can be read by both the blind and those who can see

Who was the first person to fly an airplane?

a) Wilbur Wright

b) Milton Wright

c) Orville Wright

d) Wrong-Way Corrigan

Which famous computer company did Bill Gates start?

a) Microstock
b) Google Docs
c) Microsoft
d) Macintosh

Which inventor has the most patents for his inventions?

a) Nikola Tesla
b) Orville Wright
c) Thomas Edison
d) Albert Einstein

What did Henry Ford name his first gas-powered vehicle?

a) The Edsel
b) The Quadricycle
c) The Tricycle
d) The Phonocycle

Which is not an invention created by Ben Franklin?

a) The glass harmonica
b) The kite
c) Bifocal glasses
d) The Franklin stove

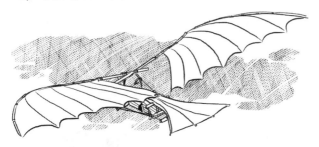

Where did Wilbur and Orville Wright first fly their airplane?

a) Dayton, Ohio
b) Puppy Hawk, North Carolina
c) Kitty Eagle, South Carolina
d) Kitty Hawk, North Carolina

What device did Thomas Edison invent to record and play back sound for the first time?

a) The cell phone
b) The phonograph
c) The telegraph
d) The kinetoscope

What famous inventor encouraged Henry Ford to continue working on his gas-powered engine?

a) Alexander Graham Bell
b) Thomas Edison
c) Claude Monet
d) Bill Gates

What power source did Nikola Tesla experiment with?

a) Electricity
b) Steam
c) Batteries
d) Nuclear power

Which of these is Thomas Edison's most famous invention?

a) The electronic back massager
b) The electric lightbulb
c) The record player
d) The computer

Who was the famous US inventor who competed with Nikola Tesla to be the first to deliver electricity to people's homes?

a) Albert Einstein
b) Wilbur Wright
c) Leonardo da Vinci
d) Thomas Edison

Which of these did Ben Franklin accomplish?

a) Being governor of Pennsylvania
b) Helping to open the Pennsylvania Hospital
c) Helping to write the Declaration of Independence in Philadelphia
d) All of the above

Which of these is not one of the strategies Henry Ford used to make cars more quickly?

a) The assembly line
b) Mass production
c) The assembly triangle
d) Paying his workers more

What scientist is famous for discovering the nature of lightning?

a) Nikola Tesla
b) Albert Einstein
c) Thomas Edison
d) Ben Franklin

The Art of Trivia

They say that art is open to interpretation. Trivia questions are not. How much do you know about these extraordinary artists, designers, and architects?

What famous line did cartoonist Chuck Jones make the Road Runner say in his *Looney Toons* cartoons?

a) "Bam! Bam!"

b) "Beep! Beep!"

c) "Boop-oop-a-doop!"

d) "Bada bing! Bada boom!"

Which artist painted many self-portraits featuring their famous eyebrows?

a) Frida Kahlo

b) Andy Warhol

c) Maya Angelou

d) Elton John

What type of art is Andy Warhol known for?

a) Finger painting

b) Pop Art

c) Pottery

d) Collage

Which architect is known as the greatest American architect of all time?

a) Frank Gehry
b) Frank Lloyd Wright
c) Henry Ford
d) Frank N. Beans

Which series of Norman Rockwell paintings helped raise money to support American soliders in World War II?

a) The Four Freedoms
b) The Fantastic Four
c) The Four-Leaf Clovers
d) The Four Seasons

Frida Kahlo was the first twentieth-century female Mexican artist to have a painting hung in which famous museum?

a) The Louvre Museum in Paris
b) The Diego Rivera Hall of Fame
c) The Blue House
d) The Colosseum

What is the *Mona Lisa*?

a) A famous painting by Leonardo da Vinci
b) A character who appears from a painting in Harry Potter
c) One of Christopher Columbus's ships
d) A type of sandwich

Frank Lloyd Wright designed a house called Fallingwater.

a) True
b) False

What style of painting, featuring angular forms, made Pablo Picasso famous?

a) Surrealism
b) Realism
c) Cubism
d) Ovalism

Why did Chuck Jones create the cartoon character Private Snafu?

a) To help educate soldiers in the US Army
b) To encourage postal workers to deliver the mail fast
c) To remind members of Congress to be honest
d) To teach members of the Coast Guard to drive boats

When Frida Kahlo's doctor told her she was too sick to attend her art opening, what did she do?

  a) Canceled the art opening and took a nap
  b) Attended the opening in her bed
  c) Moved the art opening to her bedroom
  d) All of the above

What type of painter was Claude Monet?

  a) Impressionist
  b) Surrealist
  c) Stupendist
  d) Realist

What famous and funny character did Chuck Jones create?

  a) Superbunny
  b) Bugs Bunny
  c) Chewbacca
  d) Kermit

Which of the below is *not* a building designed by Frank Lloyd Wright?

  a) The Imperial Hotel
  b) Johnson Wax Administration Building
  c) The Guggenheim Museum
  d) The Empire State Building

The Royal Subjects

How much do you know about royal rulers?
Let's see if you can measure up!

How old was King Tut when he became the pharaoh of Egypt?

a) Approximately 3 years old
b) Approximately 10 years old
c) Approximately 30 years old
d) Approximately 3,000 years old

What was King Henry VIII famous for?

a) Wanting a son
b) Sentencing his enemies to death
c) Eating a lot of food
d) All of the above

What was Queen Elizabeth I's nickname?

a) The Best Bessy
b) Good Queen Bess
c) Good Ol' Bessy
d) Messy Bessy

What was one of Princess Diana's jobs before she joined the Royal Family?

a) House painter
b) Assistant kindergarten teacher
c) Pizza delivery driver
d) Cheerleader

What is the name of the celebration marking Alexandrina Victoria's sixtieth year as queen?

a) Ruby Jubilee
b) Diamond Jubilee
c) Crystal Jubilee
d) Silver Jubilee

How old was Queen Victoria when she became queen of England?

a) 8 years old
b) 18 years old
c) 28 years old
d) 88 years old

King Tut was buried in the Valley of the Kings in Egypt.

a) True
b) False

Why did King Henry VIII start the Church of England?

a) So he could get a divorce

b) Because the Vatican was too far away

c) To improve relations with Spain

d) As an excuse to throw another dinner party

What did Princess Diana do when she became famous?

a) Used her fame to raise money for charity

b) Visited victims of land mine explosions

c) Traveled the world to meet with people who suffered from serious illnesses

d) All of the above

Why was King Tut mummified after his death?

a) To be ready for Halloweeen

b) To preserve his body for the afterlife

c) To scare off thieves

d) To keep him warm in his tomb

Which queen of England helped defeat the Spanish Armada in 1588?

a) Queen Victoria

b) Queen Elizabeth I

c) Queen Diana of Scots

d) Queen Mary

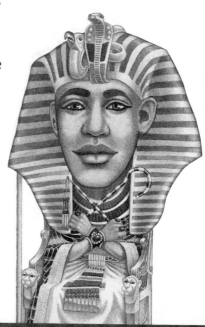

All About Activists

Activists have done so much to help so many!
But can you remember all their good deeds?

**Where did Mother Teresa do
most of her missionary work?**

a) The United States

b) Albania

c) India

d) Yugoslavia

**Who was the most
famous Latinx
American civil
rights activist?**

a) Cesar Chavez

b) Fidel Castro

c) Malala
Yousafzai

d) Gloria Steinem

**Which form of
protest was *not*
used by Gandhi?**

a) Refusal to work

b) Refusal to buy
goods

c) Refusal to eat

d) Refusal to dance

Which of these activists fought hard so that women had the right to vote?

a) Susan B. Anthony
b) Harriet Beecher Stowe
c) Harriet Tubman
d) Annie Oakley

Who won a Nobel Peace Prize for their work to end apartheid?

a) Mahatma Gandhi
b) Nelson Mandela
c) Martin Luther King Jr.
d) Coretta Scott King

Why did Gandhi march over 240 miles to the sea in 1930?

a) To protest the British tax on salt
b) To protest taking the train
c) To protest buying British textiles
d) To protest violence

Which environmental activist helped clean up New York's Hudson River?

a) Johnny Appleseed
b) Rachel Carson
c) Richard Branson
d) Pete Seeger

When Susan B. Anthony said she wanted to fight for women's suffrage, what did she mean?

a) She wanted women to get rid of their headaches.
b) She wanted women to have the right to vote.
c) She wanted to ban drinking soda.
d) All of the above

Who spent her life fighting to protect the environment?

a) Rachel Carson
b) Julia Child
c) Dolly Parton
d) Frida Kahlo

What is apartheid?

a) A river in South Africa
b) The name of Nelson Mandela's first book
c) The name of the prison where Nelson Mandela was kept
d) A political system in South Africa that was used to keep races apart

Why was Pete Seeger put on a list that prevented him from performing on television?

a) Because some people in Congress thought he was a Communist
b) Because his songs had too many banjos
c) Because his music wasn't very popular
d) Because he spoke out against war

Which social activist used peaceful protests as a way to win India's freedom from Britain?

a) Maya Angelou
b) Mahatma Gandhi
c) Harriet Tubman
d) Martin Luther King Jr.

What was the title of Rachel Carson's revolutionary book about the dangers of pesticides?

a) *Silent Spring*
b) *Better Wash that Apple*
c) *DDT and Me*
d) *Organically Speaking*

Which activist fought for the right for girls to receive an education in Pakistan?

a) Gloria Steinem
b) Sojourner Truth
c) Malala Yousafzai
d) Mother Teresa

What major prize did Martin Luther King Jr. win in 1964?

a) The New York State Lottery
b) The Nobel Peace Prize
c) The Pulitzer Prize
d) The Presidential Medal of Freedom

After serving twenty-seven years in prison, who became the first Black president of South Africa?

a) Nelson Mandela
b) Booker T. Washington
c) Jacques Cousteau
d) Mahatma Gandhi

Which famous leader influenced Martin Luther King Jr.'s ideas about peaceful protest?

a) Mother Teresa
b) Mahatma Gandhi
c) Genghis Khan
d) Julius Caesar

Why was Susan B. Anthony put in jail?

a) Because she stole a protest sign
b) Because she voted and was a woman
c) Because she went out in public without wearing bloomers
d) All of the above

Trivia by the Numbers

Here are some trivia questions that are all about numbers! But will your answers add up?

How many career hits did baseball legend Roberto Clemente have?

a) 1,000

b) 2,000

c) 3,000

d) 4,000

How far was Marco Polo's trip from Italy to China?

a) Less than 10 miles

b) Less than 100 miles

c) Less than 1,000 miles

d) Less than 100,000 miles

How old was the Dalai Lama when he was named the leader of Tibet?

a) 40 years old

b) 24 years old

c) 14 years old

d) 4 years old

Which period of time did *Julius* Caesar have named after him?

    a) The first week in January

    b) March 15 (the ides of March)

    c) The entire month of July

    d) August 1 to 15

How many home runs did Babe Ruth hit in the 1927 season?

    a) 20

    b) 30

    c) 50

    d) 60

How many gold medals did Jesse Owens win during the Summer Olympics in Berlin, Germany, in 1936?

    a) 1

    b) 4

    c) 14

    d) 40

What was the name of the mission to space that landed Neil Armstrong on the moon?

   a) Apollo 1

   b) Apollo 7

   c) Apollo 11

   d) Apollo 13

What number did Jackie Robinson wear when he played his first game for the Brooklyn Dodgers?

   a) 22

   b) 32

   c) 42

   d) 52

At the height of their empire, what percentage of the earth's population was ruled by Genghis Khan and his relatives?

   a) 10%

   b) 25%

   c) 70%

   d) 110%

What altitude did Amelia Earhart hit when she set the record for the highest flight?

a) 400 feet

b) 4,000 feet

c) 14,000 feet

d) 140,000 feet

How old was Malala Yousafzai when she won the Nobel Peace Prize?

a) 7 years old

b) 17 years old

c) 37 years old

d) 67 years old

How many World Cup titles did Pelé win?

a) 1

b) 3

c) 5

d) 1,000

When she was First Lady in 1933, how many letters did Eleanor Roosevelt receive?

a) 3
b) Over 300
c) Over 3,000
d) Over 300,000

Which of the below is the title of a paper that George Washington Carver wrote?

a) *103 Wars and Peas*
b) *21 Crop Rotation Techniques That Will Make Your Head Spin*
c) *How to Grow the Peanut: And 105 Ways of Preparing It for Human Consumption*
d) *10 Ways Peanut Butter Is Better*

How many pieces of art did Pablo Picasso create in his lifetime?

a) Over 2,000
b) Over 10,000
c) Over 25,000
d) Over 50,000

Which of the below is the correct title of one of Jules Verne's famous books?

a) *20,000 Miles from the Earth to the Black Hole*
b) *Eighty Leagues Under the Sea*
c) *Around the World in Eighty Days*
d) *Around the World in 20,000 Days*

Derek Jeter was the second player in history to reach three thousand hits with a home run.

a) True
b) False

How many plays did William Shakespeare write?

a) At least 10
b) At least 35
c) 1,564
d) 1,561,000

How old is King Tut's tomb?

a) Over 30 years old
b) Over 300 years old
c) Over 3,000 years old
d) Over 3,000,000 years old

Milton Hershey's chocolate bars only cost five cents until 1969.

a) True
b) False

How old was Wolfgang Amadeus Mozart when he played piano for the empress of Austria?

a) 6 years old
b) 16 years old
c) 26 years old
d) 46 years old

And the Trivia Award Goes To . . .

All of these amazing entertainers won awards for their work. Can *you* win the award for most correct answers?

Which famous chef published a cookbook called *Mastering the Art of French Cooking*?

a) Chef Boy-yummy
b) Julia Child
c) Julia Chow
d) Donald McDonald

What was the name of the Three Stooges' first hit film?

a) *Four Little Piglets*
b) *Boom Goes the Weasel*
c) *Men in Black*
d) *Men in Black 2*

Which of these movies was *not* made by Steven Spielberg?

a) *Jaws*
b) *Jurassic Park*
c) *E.T.*
d) *Psycho*

Steven Spielberg won his first Oscar for Best Director for which film?

    a) *Schindler's List*

    b) *The Color Purple*

    c) *Amistad*

    d) *Saving Private Ryan*

Which of these was *not* part of the Three Stooges' act when they did slapstick comedy?

    a) Pretend fighting

    b) Getting a pie in the face

    c) Pulling a rabbit out of a hat

    d) Lots of falling down

Which of these is *not* one of Alfred Hitchcock's scary movies?

    a) *Front Window*

    b) *Psycho*

    c) *Vertigo*

    d) *North by Northwest*

What was the name of Lucille Ball's famous TV show?

a) *Lucky Lucy*
b) *I Kind of Like Lucy*
c) *I Love Lucy*
d) *The Lucy and Desi Show*

What is Julia Child famous for?

a) Bringing French cooking to American audiences
b) Her amazing television personality
c) Her many cookbooks
d) All of the above

What was the name of Robert Ripley's famous cartoon that later became the inspiration for a TV show?

a) *Believe It or Not!*
b) *You Better Believe It!*
c) *Seeing Is Believing!*
d) *I Believe in You!*

Which of the below is one of Bruce Lee's famous movies?

a) *Face of Fury*
b) *Enter the Dragon*
c) *Return of the Lizard*
d) *Do You Kung-Fu?*

What was the name of Charlie Chaplin's most famous movie character?

a) Keystone the Kid

b) The Little Kid

c) The Little Tramp

d) The Little Rascal

What major event in Annie Oakley's life made her retire from Buffalo Bill's Wild West show?

a) A train accident

b) Newspapers printed untrue stories about her.

c) She lost her favorite rifle.

d) World War I

Which of the below is a famous quote from the suspense film director Alfred Hitchcock?

a) "The only way to get rid of my fears is to make films about them."

b) "It's time for *Alfred Hitchcock Presents*!"

c) "I don't like birds very much."

d) "I never take showers; only baths."

Which was one of Charlie Chaplin's famous props?

a) Ruby slippers

b) Bowler hat

c) Lightsaber

d) Bowling ball

Reading Is Believing

Not everything you read is true! Especially in these trivia questions about some of the greatest Who Was? authors.

Which famous author created the character Harry Potter?

   a) J. K. Rowling
   b) Maya Angelou
   c) Dr. Seuss
   d) Albus Dumbledore

What is Stan Lee's real name?

   a) Stanley Lieber
   b) The Human Torch
   c) Bruce Banner
   d) Jack Kirby

Which river did Mark Twain famously write about?

   a) The Nile
   b) The Mississippi
   c) The Ganges
   d) The Amazon

Which superhero *wasn't* created by Stan Lee?

   a) The Hulk

b) Iron Man

c) Spider-Man

d) Lavagirl

What job did Maya Angelou have in her long career?

a) First Black streetcar driver in San Francisco

b) Coordinator for Martin Luther King Jr.'s Leadership Conference

c) Professor at Wake Forest University

d) All of the above and also calypso dancer!

Which of these is considered Mark Twain's most important book?

a) *The Adventures of Huckleberry Finn*

b) *Tom Sawyer and the Mississippi*

c) *Tom Sawyer Goes to Town*

d) *Who Was Huck Finn?*

Which of these is *not* a character from Lewis Carroll's book *Alice in Wonderland*?

a) The Cheshire Cat

b) The White Rabbit

c) The Queen of Clubs

d) The Hatter

Which play was written by William Shakespeare?

a) *The Taming of the Newt*

b) *Romeo Meets Juliet*

c) *Hamlet and Cheese*

d) *Titus Andronicus*

What was Mark Twain's real name?

a) Samuel Clemens
b) Samuel Manzanero
c) Sam Theagle
d) Uncle Sam

Which of the below is *not* the title of a book Maurice Sendak wrote?

a) *Outside Over There*
b) *In the Night Kitchen*
c) *Higglety Pigglety Pop!*
d) *Nutcracker*

What is the title of Maya Angelou's famous autobiography?

a) *I Know Why the Caged Bird Sings*
b) *On the Pulse of Morning*
c) *Letter to My Daughter*
d) *Just Give Me a Cool Drink of Water 'fore I Diiie*

Exploring Explorers

Explorers are always searching for what's over the next horizon. Here are some questions for you to explore about these brave men and women!

Historians believe that most of Marco Polo's stories are true.

 a) True
 b) False

To prepare for being weightless in space, Sally Ride trained in a plane nicknamed . . .

 a) The Vomit
    Comet
 b) The Barf Bomber
 c) The Quick 'n'
    Queasy
 d) The High-Up
    Up-Chuck

Amelia Earhart was the first woman to fly alone across the Atlantic Ocean.

 a) True
 b) False

Ferdinand Magellan's ship, the *Victoria*, was the first ship to circumnavigate the world.

- a) True
- b) False

Which continent did Ernest Shackleton explore?

- a) Africa
- b) Antarctica
- c) New Jersey
- d) The North Pole

What was Christopher Columbus looking for when he discovered the New World?

- a) A faster route to the Indies
- b) Gold
- c) Fame and fortune
- d) All of the above

Which obstacle did Ferdinand Magellan and his crew face on his travels around the world?

- a) Starvation
- b) Scurvy
- c) Mutiny
- d) All of the above

Which ship did Christopher Columbus captain on his first trip to the New World?

- a) The *Niña*
- b) The *Pinta*
- c) The *Santa Maria*
- d) The *Queen Isabella*

Who was the first astronaut to step foot on the moon?

- a) Sally Field
- b) Neil Armstrong
- c) Buzz Aldrin
- d) Michael Collins

Which of these is *not* the name of a ship sailed by Ernest Shackleton?

a) *Endurance*
b) The *Enterprise*
c) *Nimrod*
d) *Quest*

Sally Ride is famous for being the first . . .

a) Astronaut to fly in three space shuttle missions
b) Female American astronaut
c) Tennis player in space
d) Astronaut to lose her boots in space

Which astronaut led the design team that created the space shuttle's robotic arm?

a) John Glenn
b) Marvin D. Martian
c) Han Solo
d) Sally Ride

What did Marco Polo name his book about his adventures around the world?

a) *Marco's Travel Diary*
b) *The Description of the World*
c) *Are We There Yet?*
d) *Far Away from Home*

What ocean was named by Ferdinand Magellan?

a) The Atlantic Ocean
b) The Pacific Ocean
c) The Arctic Ocean
d) The Indian Ocean

The Rules of the Game

These sports heroes racked up lots of impressive statistics during their amazing careers. Can you improve your trivia stats by answering these questions correctly?

Which African American athlete was named the top track athlete of the first half of the twentieth century?

a) Jesse Owens

b) Jackie Robinson

c) Babe Ruth

d) Muhammad Ali

Who was the first Black player on a modern major league baseball team?

a) Babe Ruth

b) Roberto Clemente

c) Jesse Owens

d) Jackie Robinson

Which nickname was used for Wayne Gretzky?

a) The Best One

b) The One and Only

c) Puck Master

d) The Great One

What team did Roberto Clemente play for when they won the World Series in 1960?

a) The Brooklyn Dodgers
b) The Pittsburgh Pirates
c) The San Diego Padres
d) The San Francisco Giants

Who won the gold medal in 1960 for boxing in the light heavyweight division?

a) Mahatma Gandhi
b) Muhammad Ali
c) Jesse Owens
d) Roberto Clemente

What team did Babe Ruth help bring to their first World Series?

a) The Baltimore Orioles
b) The Boston Red Sox
c) The New York Mets
d) The New York Yankees

Which of the Williams sisters has won more Olympic gold medals?

a) Venus

b) Serena

c) As of the year 2021, they are tied.

d) Neither sister has won a gold medal

What team did Wayne Gretzky play for when he retired from hockey?

a) The New York Rangers

b) The St. Louis Blues

c) The Edmonton Oilers

d) The Indianapolis Racers

Which baseball player was named Rookie of the Year after his first Major League season?

a) Joe DiMaggio

b) Babe Ruth

c) Derek Jeter

d) Roberto Clemente

What position did Michael Jordan play for the University of North Carolina Tar Heels?

a) Quarterback
b) Point guard
c) Small forward
d) Shooting guard

Why was the 2000 World Series called the Subway Series?

a) Because Derek Jeter took the subway to the games
b) Because the New York Mets and New York Yankees competed against each other and fans could ride the subway to the series games
c) Because the parking lot at Yankee Stadium was full every night
d) Because it was the 100th anniversary of the New York City Subway

What award did Serena Williams win in 2015?

a) Best Sister Award
b) *Sports Illustrated* Sportsperson of the Year
c) A Grammy for Best Song
d) Best Dressed at Wimbledon

What NBA team recruited Michael Jordan to play basketball?

a) The New York Knicks
b) The Chicago Bulls
c) The Houston Starships
d) The Portland Trailblazers

Pelé was famous for playing in which position on the soccer team?

a) Captain
b) Forward
c) Midfielder
d) Quarterback

What baseball team did Derek Jeter play for?

a) The New York Yankees
b) The New York Yankees
c) The New York Yankees
d) All of the above. Derek LOVES the Yankees!

What did Michael Jordan do when he won his first gold medal at the Olympics?

a) Gave it to his mother
b) Made it into a belt buckle
c) Melted it down
d) Stored it in a secret safe

What other job did Pelé do besides playing soccer?

a) Soldier in the Brazilian army
b) Shoe shiner
c) Brazil's Minister of Sport
d) All of the above

True Trailblazers

These brave people forged their own path through life! Are you brave enough to find your way to the correct answers to these trivia questions?

How did Alexander Hamilton die?

a) He got yellow fever.

b) He was shot during a duel with Aaron Burr.

c) He slipped and fell while performing in a musical.

d) He was shot by a British soldier during the American Revolution.

Who was the first Latina US Supreme Court justice?

a) Ruth Bader Ginsburg

b) Michelle Obama

c) Sonia Sotomayor

d) Celia Cruz

Which female member of the Shoshone tribe made Lewis and Clark's journey to the Pacific Ocean a success?

a) Pomp

b) Sacagawea

c) Bitterroots

d) Maria Tallchief

Which of these is one of Frederick Douglass's great accomplishments?

a) Taught himself to read and write
b) Escaped from slavery dressed as a sailor
c) Campaigned for President Abraham Lincoln
d) All of the above

Why was Harriet Tubman given the nickname "Moses"?

a) Because she liked to read the Bible
b) Because she led so many people to freedom
c) Because that was her father's name
d) Because she needed a secret code name

As the spiritual leader of Tibetan Buddhism, what important message did the Dalai Lama give to the world?

a) Work hard and you can get rich.
b) Be compassionate.
c) Don't talk to strangers.
d) Eat a balanced diet.

Which former enslaved person was responsible for building the Tuskegee Normal School?

   a) George Washington Carver
   b) Booker T. Washington
   c) Harriet Tubman
   d) Ida B. Wells

Which pioneer died defending the Alamo in Texas?

   a) Daniel Boone
   b) Annie Oakley
   c) Davy Crockett
   d) Johnny Appleseed

Who was responsible for saving French cities from the English when she was only a teenager?

   a) Catherine the Great
   b) Joan of Arc
   c) Queen Elizabeth I
   d) Marie Antoinette

Why did Johnny Appleseed plant so many apple trees?

a) To help pioneer families
b) To prevent apple trees from going extinct
c) To get famous
d) All of the above

Why did Paul Revere ride to Lexington, Massachusetts, on April 18, 1775?

a) To pick up groceries
b) To see how fast his horse was
c) To warn the citizens of oncoming British troops
d) To audition for the Pony Express

What was Maria Tallchief's real last name?

a) Russe
b) Osage
c) Porter
d) Tall Chief is her real last name. She refused to change it!

How did Joan of Arc disguise her appearance?

a) By traveling inside a giant wooden horse
b) By wearing a fake moustache
c) By dressing as a boy
d) By changing her name to King Charles

Which nickname was used for David Crockett?

a) Colonel
b) The Gentleman from the Cane
c) Davy
d) All of the above

Which chief led many American Indian tribes in their quest to protect their lands and way of life?

a) Returns Again
b) Sitting Bull
c) Mixed Day
d) Four Robes

Presidential Questions

All of these US presidents were voted into office by the American people. But can you vote for the right answers to these trivia questions?

Which founding father of the United States has his face carved into Mount Rushmore?

a) Alexander Hamilton
b) John Quincy Adams
c) Barack Obama
d) Thomas Jefferson

Which of these were some of Barack Obama's accomplishments as president?

a) Restoring relations with Cuba
b) Providing more Americans with affordable health care
c) Creating more than 10 million jobs
d) All of the above

Who was General George Washington's assistant during the Revolutionary War?

a) Aaron Burr
b) General Cornwallis
c) James Madison
d) Alexander Hamilton

Before becoming president, Barack Obama was a senator from . . .

a) Indiana
b) Hawaii
c) Illinois
d) Cuba

Which Civil War general later became president of the United States?

a) Robert E. Lee
b) Ulysses S. Grant
c) Abraham Lincoln
d) George Washington

How did Theodore Roosevelt first become president of the United States?

a) He barely won the election!
b) He won the election in a landslide victory!
c) He took over when President McKinley was assassinated.
d) The Supreme Court picked his name out of a hat.

Which of the below is a true fact about Alexander Hamilton?

a) He was the first secretary of the treasury in the United States
b) He wanted the British to win the Revolutionary War
c) He spoke Russian
d) He was best friends with Aaron Burr

Which American president is credited for starting the fight to end slavery?

a) George Washington
b) Abraham Lincoln
c) Thomas Jefferson
d) Ulysses S. Grant

What was one of Franklin Roosevelt's greatest accomplishments?

a) Helping to start the Great Depression
b) Guiding the United States toward victory in World War II
c) Canceling the New Deal
d) All of the above

Alexander Hamilton was the second vice president of the United States.

a) True
b) False

Which of these is *not* a hashtag that could describe Barack Obama?

a) #MyfamilycallsmeBarry
b) #NoDramaObama
c) #HawaiianPOTUS
d) #1TermPresident

Which US president promised to land an American astronaut on the moon?

a) Lyndon Johnson
b) Richard Nixon
c) Ronald Reagan
d) John F. Kennedy

Musical Notes

They say it's easier to remember something
if you sing a song about it. Find out if that's
true by singing the correct answers to these
questions about famous musicians!

**Which nickname is sometimes used to describe
Bruce Springsteen?**

a) The King

b) The Boss

c) The Star

d) The E Street Singer

**Which musical genius composed the opera
The Marriage of Figaro?**

a) Lorenzo Da Ponte

b) Figaro

c) Wolfgang Amadeus
Mozart

d) Jim Henson

**Why was it hard for Selena
to sing songs in Spanish
when she first started her
career?**

a) The notes were too high.

b) She didn't speak
Spanish.

c) The songs didn't rhyme.

d) She was tone-deaf.

What type of music did Bob Marley help make popular?

a) Calypso
b) Reggae
c) Rap
d) Ska

Who wrote the music for Disney's *The Lion King*?

a) Walt Disney
b) Jim Henson
c) Elton John
d) Dolly Parton

Which of these musicians is famous for playing the trumpet?

a) Selena
b) John Lennon
c) Louis Armstrong
d) Elvis Presley

Which singer is known as the King of Rock 'n' Roll?

a) Elvis Presley
b) Mick Jagger
c) Elton John
d) Dwayne "the Rock" Johnson

Why do many people think the Beatles chose such an unusual name for their band?

a) Because they liked bugs

b) Because their songs had a good beat

c) Because it rhymed with Feetles

d) Because "the Mop Tops" was already taken

What type of music did Aretha Franklin sing when she had her first hit record?

a) Disco

b) Rap

c) Soul

d) Country

What was the name of the first recording studio to hire Stevie Wonder?

a) Yourtown

b) Motown

c) Mytown

d) Facetown

Which famous musician was born with the name Robert Zimmerman?

a) Bob Dylan
b) Elton John
c) Mick Jagger
d) Bob Marley

What country was Bob Marley from?

a) The United Kingdom
b) Britain
c) England
d) Jamaica

Which song helped make the Beatles world-famous?

a) "Today"
b) "Yesterday"
c) "Tomorrow"
d) All of the above

Who is the lead singer of the Rolling Stones?

a) Mick Jagger
b) Elton John
c) Oliver Stone
d) Charlie Watts

Bob Marley was influenced by the beliefs of the Rastafari religion.

a) True
b) False

Which is *not* the title of a song written by Stevie Wonder?

a) "Shoo-Be-Doo-Be-Doo-Da-Day"
b) "The Hokey Pokey"
c) "Yester-me, Yester-you, Yesterday"
d) All of the above

What type of music made Dolly Parton famous?

a) Rap
b) Country
c) Disco
d) Reggae

Which nickname was often used to describe Louis Armstrong?

a) The Trumpet King
b) Satchmo
c) Super Cheeks
d) Louis the Great

Why did Bono and U2 perform at Live Aid?

a) To advertise a new type of sports beverage
b) To raise money for starving people in Ethiopia
c) To get famous
d) To be on television

Who awarded Stevie Wonder his Medal of Honor?

a) B.B. King
b) President Barack Obama
c) Ray Charles
d) The president of Motown Records

Bono is a musician from Ireland who cares deeply about justice for people around the world.

a) True
b) False

Which of the below is a famous line from a Rolling Stones song?

a) "I can't get no satisfaction"
b) "I can't get no ice cream"
c) "I can't get to the train station"
d) "I can't get this song out of my head"

Notable Names

These notable people led unforgettable lives. But can you remember all the details about what they did?

Which historical event did Paul Revere *not* participate in?

a) The Boston Tea Party

b) The American Revolution

c) The Boston Massacre

d) The Boston Cream Pie Eating Contest

Which important act did David Crockett vote against when he was in Congress?

a) Civil Rights Act of 1957

b) The Indian Removal Act

c) The Alamo Act

d) All of the above

What did Coretta Scott King do to help the fight for civil rights?

a) Served as a delegate to an international peace conference

b) Led a protest march in Memphis, Tennessee

c) Held a Freedom Concert in New York City

d) All of the above

What national holiday did Coretta Scott King campaign to have created?

  a) Martin Luther King Jr. Day
  b) Flag Day
  c) Memorial Day
  d) Labor Day

Why did Daniel Boone and many other settlers move west?

  a) To own land of their own
  b) To give their horses some exercise
  c) For the views of the Mississippi River
  d) To escape from hungry bears

According to legend, who is the creator of the first American flag?

  a) Abigail Adams
  b) Fanny Flag
  c) Betsy Ross
  d) Martha Washington

Who is responsible for carving the Wilderness Road to Kentucky?

a) Daniel Boone
b) Booker T. Washington
c) Abraham Lincoln
d) Davy Crockett

Sonia Sotomayor attended Princeton University.

a) True
b) False

Which president nominated Sonia Sotomayor to the Supreme Court?

a) George Washington
b) Barack Obama
c) George Bush
d) Ronald Reagan

Helen Keller was the first blind-deaf woman to graduate from college.

a) True
b) False

Which of the below is a famous Native American ballet dancer?

a) Sonya Sotomayor
b) Maria Tallchief
c) Sacagawea
d) Oprah Winfrey

Which historical figure was made famous thanks to a poem by Henry Wadsworth Longfellow?

a) Thomas Jefferson
b) Paul Revere
c) Johnny Appleseed
d) Davy Crockett

What is one of Maria Tallchief's greatest accomplishments?

a) She was America's first prima ballerina.
b) She was the first woman to do ballet in space.
c) She invented ballet.
d) She starred in the movie *Presenting Ballet Betty*.

Which of the below did Betsy Ross *not* sew to help the Continental Army defeat the British?

a) Blankets
b) Flags
c) Tents
d) Beach towels

What important issue did Sonia Sotomayor make a ruling on in 1995?

a) The Major League Baseball strike
b) The legalization of same-sex marriage
c) The building of Hoover Dam
d) The need for more hot dog carts in New York City

According to legend, who told Joan of Arc to save France?

a) Her father
b) An angel
c) The king of France
d) A talking cow

Who escaped slavery and delivered many others to freedom using the Underground Railroad?

a) Harriet Beecher Stowe
b) Harriet Tubman
c) Booker T. Washington
d) George Washington Carver

Booker T. Washington received an honorary degree from Harvard University in 1896.

a) True
b) False

Fact or Fiction?

Can you tell which facts about these famous authors are actually fiction?

Which pair of brothers worked together for their whole lives and are known for retelling fairy tales?

   a) The Wright Brothers
   b) The Brothers Grimm
   c) The Seuss Brothers
   d) The Rumpelstiltskin Brothers

Jeff Kinney's lead character from *Diary of a Wimpy Kid* became a float in the Macy's Thanksgiving Day Parade in 2010.

   a) True
   b) False

Which author wrote *Pride and Prejudice* and other popular novels?

   a) Jane Seymour
   b) Jane Austen
   c) Helen Keller
   d) Gloria Steinem

Jules Verne is known for writing what type of books?

a) Science fiction
b) Romance
c) Comics
d) Cookbooks

Which book by Harriet Beecher Stowe helped spark the end of slavery in America?

a) *Uncle Tom's Cabin*
b) *The Emancipation Proclamation*
c) *I Know Why the Caged Bird Sings*
d) *House and Home Papers*

Judy Blume has worked hard to fight against . . .

a) Global warming
b) Censorship
c) Poor grammar
d) Libraries

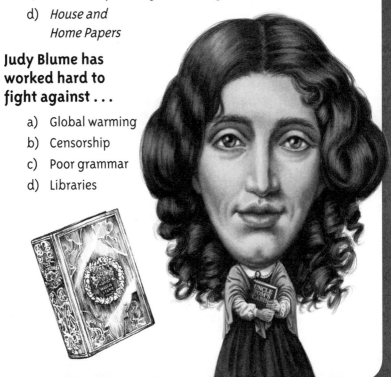

Which author wrote about her life growing up in a pioneer family?

a) Laura Ingalls Wilder
b) Nancy Drew
c) Greta Thunberg
d) Maya Angelou

Which author wrote *The Tale of Peter Rabbit*?

a) Peter the Great
b) Beatrix Potter
c) Maurice Sendak
d) Maya Angelou

Who wrote the book *Alice in Wonderland*?

a) Mark Twain
b) Lewis Carroll
c) Carroll Lewis
d) William Shakespeare

Which author is known for writing many beloved books, including one featuring a middle child dressed as a green kangaroo?

a) J. K. Rowling
b) Judy Blume
c) Maya Angelou
d) Sally Ride

Which author's books rhyme all of the time?

a) Roald Dahl
b) George Washington Carver
c) Stan Lee
d) Dr. Seuss

Before becoming a famous author, what did Beatrix Potter write about when she studied to be a scientist?

a) Mushrooms
b) Clouds
c) Rabbits
d) Farming

Why did some people try to ban J. K. Rowling's books?

a) Because they were too long
b) Because they were about magic
c) Because they had British words in them
d) Because she was a female writer

Who wrote *Where the Wild Things Are*?

a) Edgar Allan Poe
b) A monster named Moishe
c) Mark Twain
d) Maurice Sendak

Dr. Seuss's real name is Theodor Geisel.

a) True
b) False

What did Beatrix Potter do to keep people from reading her journal?

  a) Hid it in a safe
  b) Put a lock on it
  c) Fed it to a rabbit
  d) Wrote in secret code

What was Stan Lee's first job in comic books?

  a) Superhero model
  b) Gofer (office assistant)
  c) Publisher
  d) Window washer

Which of the below is *not* a phrase written by Shakespeare?

  a) "All the world's an oyster."
  b) "Parting is such sweet sorrow."
  c) "To thine own self be true."
  d) "Knock, knock! Who's there?"

Big Business

These entrepreneurs and visionaries created huge businesses that have shaped our culture. But was their impact big enough for you to remember the answers to these questions?

Oprah Winfrey is the owner of which TV network?

a) NBC
b) OWN
c) Nickelodeon
d) PBS

What did P. T. Barnum call his circus?

a) The Biggest Big Top
b) The Greatest Show on Earth
c) Jumbo's Jumbo Circus
d) Three Rings o' Fun

Why did Steve Jobs name his computer company "Apple"?

a) The name Grapes was already taken.
b) It was a commentary on the story of Adam and Eve.
c) He liked eating apples.
d) Because of the saying "Apples don't fall far from the tree"

Which business tycoon is known for his fashion *and* his support for humanitarian causes?

- a) Richard Branson
- b) Ralph Lauren
- c) Robert Ripley
- d) Elton John

What was Walt Disney's first full-length animated movie?

- a) *Finding Nemo*
- b) *Snow White*
- c) *The Tiger King*
- d) *Mary Stockings*

Which business tycoon began his career selling horseradish from a wooden cart?

- a) Milton Bradley
- b) Richard Branson
- c) H. J. Heinz
- d) Milton Hershey

Which adventure-seeking billionaire crossed the Atlantic Ocean in a hot-air balloon?

a) Steve Jobs
b) Jacques Cousteau
c) Richard Branson
d) Bill Gates

Why did Milton Hershey build the town of Hershey, Pennsylvania?

a) So he could be mayor
b) So he could build an amusement park
c) So his employees could have a comfortable place to live
d) So he could make his chocolate bars more famous

Which of the below was *not* part of Walt Disney's design for Disneyland?

a) Adventureland
b) Fantasyland
c) Tomorrowland
d) Farmland

Which of the below was *not* an act in one of P. T. Barnum's shows?

    a) The bearded lady
    b) Tom Thumb
    c) The Feejee Mermaid
    d) A living dinosaur

Which TV host is known as the Queen of All Media?

    a) Barbara Walters
    b) Oprah Winfrey
    c) Dolly Parton
    d) Gayle King

Who is credited for creating the character Mickey Mouse?

    a) Walt Disney
    b) Roy Disney
    c) Donald Duck
    d) Elias Disney

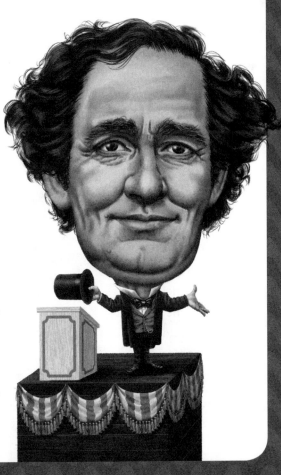

At the 1964 World's Fair, Walt Disney debuted an animatronic version of Abraham Lincoln.

a) True
b) False

What was carried by P. T. Barnum's circus trains?

a) Circus animals and performers
b) Food and supplies
c) The circus tent
d) All of the above

Who was the owner of the first factory that made ketchup without chemical preservatives?

a) Milton Hershey
b) H. J. Heinz
c) J. H. Heinz
d) Theodore Roosevelt

Bonus Pet Trivia

Some of these questions are cute and fuzzy, but others have the bite of an alligator! Good luck!

Which pet did Selena and her husband have?

a) Dogs

b) A python

c) Fish that lived in a tank built into their bed

d) All of the above

Which horse was named the 1938 Horse of the Year?

a) War Admiral

b) Man o' War

c) Rocking horse

d) Seabiscuit

What type of pet did Steve Irwin get when he was six years old?

a) A python

b) A kitten

c) A rock

d) A penguin

Which of the below did *not* help Seabiscuit become famous?

a) Starring in movies

b) Being written about in books

c) Signing autographs with his hoof

d) Appearing at birthday parties

Bucephalus was the name of Alexander the Great's trusty . . .

a) Dog
b) Goldfish
c) Horse
d) Chicken

What type of horse was Seabiscuit?

a) A pony
b) A unicorn
c) A thoroughbred
d) A Clydesdale

What Alfred Hitchcock film used trick photography to scare audiences into believing a town was being attacked by animals?

a) *The Wolves*
b) *The Birds*
c) *The Sharks*
d) *The Squirrels*

When Hillary Clinton lived in the White House, what was her cat's name?

a) Buttons
b) Socks
c) Suspenders
d) Hats

Answer Key

Page 4
c) To inspire children to exercise
d) All of the above
b) FLOTUS

Page 5
b) Become the Democratic nominee for president
b) The Reservoir in Central Park
d) The War of the Tulips
b) To restore historic artifacts and put them on display

Page 6
c) Abigail Adams
a) Betty Ford
d) The need for a transcontinental railway
b) Strelka

Page 7
c) "Float like a butterfly, sting like a bee."
d) "That's one small step for a man, one giant leap for mankind."
c) "I came, I saw, I conquered."
a) "I refuse to settle for something less than great."

Page 8
b) "I believe that with great wealth comes great responsibility—a responsibility to give back to society."
c) "Art is what you can get at the supermarket."
b) "I have a dream . . ."
b) "Bon appétit!"

Page 9
a) "I never painted dreams. I painted my own reality."
d) "Mr. Watson—come here—I want to see you."
a) "Crikey!"
b) "The only thing we have to fear is fear itself."

Page 10
c) Vikings
b) Edward Teach
c) Jacques Cousteau

Page 11
True
b) To intimidate their enemies
a) *The Silent World*
c) Leif Erikson

Page 12
a) *The Revenge*
True
b) Along the coast of North Carolina
d) Cannon

Page 13
b) *Harry Potter and the Chamber of Gems*
c) *Little House on the Prairie*
c) Roald Dahl
True

Page 14
a) Diary of a Wimpy Kid
a) *A Christmas Carol*
d) Harriet Beecher Stowe

Page 15
b) A covered wagon
a) *James and the Rotten Peach*
a) Interviewed local people and wrote down the stories

Page 16
b) A character in a series of books by Jeff Kinney
b) *Double Chocolate Fudge*
c) *Blue Eggs and Bacon*

Page 17
b) Charles Darwin
a) Whooping cough
b) Sir Isaac Newton

Page 18
a) *A Brief History of Time*
True
b) Albert Einstein

Page 19
d) Galileo
a) Poland
d) All of the above
b) Radium

Page 20
a) Albert Einstein
c) The Galapagos
b) The Plague
True

Page 21
c) Rainbows
a) Marie Curie
a) George Washington Carver
b) That animals and plants evolve slowly over time

Page 22
b) Movies that play sound and images on the screen together
d) *The Empire Strikes Back*
c) Princess Leia

Page 23
b) Robert Ripley
d) Shooting a target while swimming underwater
a) To protect himself
b) *The Crocodile Hunter*

Page 24
b) Industrial Light & Magic
d) All of the above
d) Harry Houdini
c) The Vanishing Elephant Trick

Page 25
c) To be the first person to fly a plane in Australia
b) Harrison Ford
d) "May the Force be with you."
d) Squiggles

Page 26
c) Fidel Castro
b) The Tuskegee Airmen
b) Winston Churchill

Page 27
c) Napoleon Bonaparte
d) All of the above
b) Fresno

Page 28
a) He was the first Black pilot to shoot down a German war plane.
c) Alexandria (by Alexander the Great)
a) To establish that all male citizens of France were equal under the law

Page 29
a) Nikola Tesla
d) A form of the alphabet designed by Louis Braille that can be read by both the blind and those who can see
c) Orville Wright

Page 30
c) Microsoft
c) Thomas Edison
b) The Quadricycle

Page 31
b) The kite
d) Kitty Hawk, North Carolina
b) The phonograph

Page 32
b) Thomas Edison
a) Electricity
b) The electric lightbulb

Page 33
d) Thomas Edison
d) All of the above
c) The assembly triangle
d) Ben Franklin

Page 34
b) Beep! Beep!
a) Frida Kahlo
b) Pop Art

Page 35
b) Frank Lloyd Wright
a) The Four Freedoms
a) The Louvre Museum in Paris

Page 36
a) A famous painting by Leonardo da Vinci
True
c) Cubism
a) To help educate soldiers in the US Army

Page 37
b) Attended the opening in her bed
a) Impressionist
b) Bugs Bunny
d) The Empire State Building

Page 38
b) Approximately 10 years old
d) All of the above
b) Good Queen Bess

Page 39
b) Assistant kindergarten teacher
b) Diamond Jubilee
b) 18 years old
True

Page 40
a) So he could get a divorce
d) All of the above
b) To preserve his body for the afterlife
b) Queen Elizabeth I

Page 41
c) India
a) Cesar Chavez
d) Refusal to dance

Page 42
a) Susan B. Anthony
b) Nelson Mandela
a) To protest the British tax on salt

Page 43
d) Pete Seeger
b) She wanted women to have the right to vote.
a) Rachel Carson

Page 44
d) A political system in South Africa that was used to keep races apart
a) Because some people in Congress thought he was a Communist
b) Mahatma Gandhi

Page 45
a) *Silent Spring*
c) Malala Yousafzai
b) The Nobel Peace Prize

Page 46
a) Nelson Mandela
b) Mahatma Gandhi
b) Because she voted and was a woman

Page 47
c) 3,000
b) Less than 100,000 miles
d) 4 years old

Page 48
c) The entire month of July
d) 60
b) 4

Page 49
c) Apollo 11
c) 42
b) 25%

Page 50
c) 14,000 feet
b) 17 years old
b) 3

Page 51
d) Over 300,000
c) *How to Grow the Peanut: And 105 Ways of Preparing It for Human Consumption*
d) Over 50,000

Page 52
c) *Around the World in Eighty Days*
True
b) At least 35

Page 53
c) Over 3,000 years old
True
a) 6 years old

Page 54
b) Julia Child
c) *Men in Black*
d) *Psycho*

Page 55
a) *Schindler's List*
c) Pulling a rabbit out of a hat
a) *Front Window*

Page 56
c) *I Love Lucy*
d) All of the above
a) *Believe It or Not!*
b) *Enter the Dragon*

Page 57
c) The Little Tramp
a) A train accident
a) "The only way to get rid of my fears is to make films about them."
b) Bowler hat

Page 58
a) J. K. Rowling
a) Stanley Lieber
b) The Mississippi
d) Lavagirl

Page 59
d) All of the above and also calypso dancer!
a) *The Adventures of Huckleberry Finn*
c) The Queen of Clubs
d) *Titus Andronicus*

Page 60
a) Samuel Clemens
d) *Nutcracker*
a) *I Know Why the Caged Bird Sings*

Page 61
False
a) The Vomit Comet
True

Page 62
True
b) Antarctica
d) All of the above

Page 63
d) All of the above
c) The *Santa Maria*
b) Neil Armstrong

Page 64
b) The *Enterprise*
b) Female American astronaut
d) Sally Ride

Page 65
b) *The Description of the World*
b) The Pacific Ocean

Page 66
a) Jesse Owens
d) Jackie Robinson
d) The Great One

Page 67
b) The Pittsburgh Pirates
b) Muhammad Ali
d) The New York Yankees

Page 68
c) As of the year 2021, they are tied.
a) The New York Rangers
c) Derek Jeter

Page 69
d) Shooting guard
b) Because the New York Mets and New York Yankees competed against each other and fans could ride the subway to the series games
b) *Sports Illustrated* Sportsperson of the Year

Page 70
b) The Chicago Bulls
b) Forward
d) All of the above. Derek LOVES the Yankees!

Page 71
a) Gave it to his mother
d) All of the above

Page 72
b) He was shot during a duel with Aaron Burr.
c) Sonia Sotomayor
b) Sacagawea

Page 73
d) All of the above
b) Because she led so many people to freedom
b) Be compassionate.

Page 74
b) Booker T. Washington
c) Davy Crockett
b) Joan of Arc

Page 75
a) To help pioneer families
c) To warn the citizens of oncoming British troops
d) Tall Chief is her real last name. She refused to change it!

Page 76
c) By dressing as a boy
d) All of the above
b) Sitting Bull

Page 77
d) Thomas Jefferson
d) All of the above
d) Alexander Hamilton

Page 78
c) Illinois
b) Ulysses S. Grant
c) He took over when President McKinley was assassinated.

Page 79
a) He was the first secretary of the treasury in the United States
b) Abraham Lincoln
b) Guiding the United States toward victory in World War II

Page 80
False
d) #1TermPresident
d) John F. Kennedy

Page 81
b) The Boss
c) Wolfgang Amadeus Mozart
b) She didn't speak Spanish.

Page 82
b) Reggae
c) Elton John
c) Louis Armstrong
a) Elvis Presley

Page 83
a) Because they liked bugs
c) Soul
b) Motown

Page 84
a) Bob Dylan
d) Jamaica
b) "Yesterday"

Page 85
a) Mick Jagger
True
b) "The Hokey Pokey"

Page 86
b) Country
b) Satchmo
b) To raise money for starving people in Ethiopia

Page 87
b) President Barack Obama
True
a) "I can't get no satisfaction"

Page 88
d) The Boston Cream Pie Eating Contest
b) The Indian Removal Act
d) All of the above

Page 89
a) Martin Luther King Jr. Day
a) To own land of their own
c) Betsy Ross

Page 90
a) Daniel Boone
True
b) Barack Obama

Page 91
True
b) Maria Tallchief
b) Paul Revere

Page 92
a) She was America's first prima ballerina.
d) Beach towels
a) The Major League Baseball strike

Page 93
b) An angel
b) Harriet Tubman
True

Page 94
b) The Brothers Grimm
True
b) Jane Austen

Page 95
a) Science fiction
a) *Uncle Tom's Cabin*
b) Censorship

Page 96
a) Laura Ingalls Wilder
b) Beatrix Potter
b) Lewis Carroll

Page 97
b) Judy Blume
d) Dr. Seuss
a) Mushrooms

Page 98
b) Because they were about magic
d) Maurice Sendak
True

Page 99
d) Wrote in secret code
b) Gofer (office assistant)
a) "All the world's an oyster."

Page 100
b) OWN
b) The Greatest Show on Earth
c) He liked eating apples.

Page 101
b) Ralph Lauren
b) *Snow White*
c) H. J. Heinz

Page 102
c) Richard Branson
c) So his employees could have a
comfortable place to live
d) Farmland

Page 103
d) A living dinosaur
b) Oprah Winfrey
a) Walt Disney

Page 104
True
d) All of the above
b) H. J. Heinz

Page 105
d) All of the above
d) Seabiscuit
a) A python
d) Appearing at birthday parties

Page 106
c) Horse
c) A thoroughbred
b) *The Birds*
b) Socks